HOW TO
GET THAT
JOB !

HOW TO GET THAT JOB!

The essential guide for today's jobseekers

Lorraine Mills

Matador
BUSINESS

Matador
5 Weir Road
Kibworth Beauchamp
Leicester LE8 0LQ UK
Tel: 0116 279 2299
Email: books@troubador.co.uk
Web: www.troubador.co.uk/matador

ISBN 978-1848762-183

A Cataloguing-in-Publication (CIP) catalogue record for this book
is available from the British Library.

This book is intended to offer advice. It is not intended to guarantee that if the
advice is followed that a reader will obtain a position applied for. Neither the
author nor publisher can be held responsible should the advice in this
book be followed but any position applied for is not forthcoming.
Note that all names and examples given are fictitious. Any resemblance to
any real person is purely coincidental.

Typeset in 11pt Book Antiqua by Troubador Publishing Ltd, Leicester, UK
Printed in the UK by TJ International, Padstow, Cornwall

Matador Business is an imprint of Troubador Publishing Ltd

To Marcus and Paul with love

Special thanks to Yvonne

Contents

Introduction

Job interviews are time consuming both for the interviewer and for you the interviewee.

So, why not get your interview technique right first time round by following these useful do's and don'ts. This will hopefully give you an extremely good chance of securing one of the positions you are applying for.

Interviews can often be quite expensive for the interviewee.

There is the cost of purchasing a suitable interview suit, which these days you are less likely to wear on a regular basis for work because most people in the work place 'dress down'. There is also the cost of dry cleaning and maintaining your interview outfit.

Travel to and from an interview can be very costly. Sometimes two or three round trips can be made to just one company and if you are unsuccessful, the whole process will have to be repeated time and time again before a position is secured.

Interviews are also very stressful so what is the point of putting yourself into a stressful and nerve wracking situation repeatedly because you choose not to improve your presentation and interview techniques?

You know you can get and do the job. You want the job so why give the opportunity of getting the job to another candidate?

Work hard to get the job by following the suggested rules and go to your interview with **PURPOSE**.

Be:
Punctual
Up to date
Reassured
Prepared
Organised
Smart
Enthusiastic

And..........**GET THAT JOB!**

This book is only a guideline to job hunting. It is down to personal choice as to how you decide to present yourself and your CV when it comes to looking for a new position.

1

Your curriculum vitae is your ticket to an interview

The content and presentation of your CV needs to be of a very high standard.

If a poor quality CV is sent out to a company it will be on the record, thanks to the power of technology. This will make it difficult for you to reapply for the role with a better CV at a later date.

So, get your CV right first time.

It may seem like an obvious thing to mention but spelling mistakes in a CV are a disaster. If you have any number of spelling mistakes in your CV, the chances of being invited for an interview will be slight.

Some of the most common spelling mistakes found in a CV

For example bussiness instead of business, stationary instead of stationery, curriculam instead of curriculum, grammer instead of grammar. The list is endless.

As a precaution, let someone you know and trust go through your CV with you before it is sent out.

A two page CV *for an experienced applicant* is more likely to hold the interest of the person who is hiring.

A one page CV can be sufficient for a very *junior level applicant*.

Mention modules if they link in with the role you are applying for.

For example, if you studied finance but some of your modules covered marketing then this would be good to mention if you are applying for a marketing role especially if the position is within a non-financial organisation.

In other words – turn your CV so it is relevant to the position you are applying for or the next role you want to do.

Detail what you actually do in your role. Bullet points are good to use but there can sometimes be a danger that, whilst the point is being put across, a short cut version of duties can indicate limited experience. So use bullet points carefully.

When it comes to outlining work experience in your CV, target the areas that you know will help get you to the next level.

If you are a graduate with limited work experience or fresh out of university looking for your first job, think about what you want out of your job and also what you have to offer.

2

CV profile

- A profile can be very important if you don't have totally relevant experience regarding the job you are applying for or if your work experience is a bit 'all over the place'.

- Include a profile on the first page.

- Ideally, he profile shouldn't be more than four lines long.

- The profile on your CV should indicate your passion for your chosen industry.

There can often be a crossover when it comes to certain industries, however your profile needs to be precise. So, if you are applying for a marketing position, stipulate marketing in your profile. If you are applying for a PR role then stipulate PR in your profile. It may be worth having three versions of virtually the same CV but with the relevant profile at the top of the first page. This will enhance your chances of at least getting offered an interview. After all, what is the point of sending a CV for a marketing position that has a profile header indicating your passion to get into PR?

- Your profile should indicate your dedication to your chosen subject, and why you feel you would be a good employee for the post.

- The profile should reflect the type of role you are actually seeking.

- Certain words and phrases, if appropriate, are a plus to mention, for example: hardworking, focused, dedicated, committed, team player with the ability to also work unsupervised, quick learner.

Let's say you studied English or Geography at university and you are seeking a marketing position, but all of the holiday jobs you held whilst at school and university were within the retail sector. For example, cashier work at WH Smiths or Boots. You have this fabulous degree that doesn't have a hint of marketing about it. This is where having a profile on your CV can be very useful.

In your profile, talk about what sort of marketing position you are looking for and the sort of personality you have.

- For example your profile could read:

  'Ambitious, hardworking graduate with a keen interest in marketing determined to secure an account executive position within a progressive marketing agency. Fast learner with excellent people skills and the ability to work as part of a team'.

4

- The profile doesn't necessarily have to be about what you have done because what you have done previously in a job may not be what you want to carry on doing.

- Use a good, strong profile if you lack experience in the area you are approaching.

- Even though you may have many years' worth of experience, a good, sharp profile may still apply, emphasising your title and indicating where your current strengths lie.

  For example:

  Marketing Account Manager with excellent skills in...

  Or:

  PR Account Director with strong exposure to......

3

CV content

If you have been out of college or university for say a year and after several temporary roles you decide on your chosen career, how on earth do you persuade a company to give you a chance and employ you?

Well, the first opportunity you may have of persuading a company to invite you in for an interview will be with a CV that gets the point across and projects who you are, what you have to offer and the sort of role you are seeking.

- Your qualifications are probably going to be on the front page of your CV.

- A good strong profile will be of great importance because it will support your experience or lack of experience.

- It is your choice if you decide to include your date of birth on your CV.

It is always a good idea to look into evening or distance learning courses that may be relevant to your chosen area of work as they could add weight to your application.

- The main body of your CV should contain your work experience.

- If you studied business at university and you are applying for a marketing post then put down the modules you studied if they include marketing.

- Also, the work experience gained during an industrial work placement is vital, so mention as much as you can because this will boost your CV content. That will be most important especially if you have recently graduated.

Having said this, you may find that after four years in the workplace your CV is going off on a tangent and you may wish to focus more on what you originally studied. For this reason, you may need to refer to the experience gained during an industrial placement.

- IT skills should be mentioned under a separate heading.

- Hobbies and interests outside the workplace are always vital to put down on a CV as they can create more of a conversation between the interviewer and the interviewee.

If you are posting or emailing your CV, put your name in small type on the bottom of the second (and third!) page(s) so it doesn't get confused with a CV belonging to someone else.

- Dangerous and antisocial sports are not a good

idea to mention on a CV.

- Avoid talking about travel and being 'passionate' about travel. This may indicate that you are a bit of a 'fly-by-night' and that after six months you'll be off trekking the Himalayas again!

- Avoid talking about clubbing, socialising with friends, gigs, etc. as this might indicate that you will roll into work the next day in an unfit state unable to do your job properly, and that you could be unreliable.

Also, try not to mention too many interests as this may give the impression that you will be distracted from doing the job you are applying for.

For example, if you are committed to doing evening and weekend work elsewhere, what will happen if there is a deadline to meet at your main place of work and you need to do extra hours?

Full reference details are not always a good idea to mention on a CV.

Applicants sometimes mention their present employer's contact details in a CV. This is not a good idea if your boss doesn't know that you are looking for a new job!

- 'References available upon request' is the best way to end a CV. This will also mean that if the names of your contacts change you will not have to make any amendments to your CV.

As mentioned before, always, always, check your CV for spelling mistakes and typos. The number of CVs that slip through the net with spelling mistakes can be quite alarming. Make sure you are not submitting one of those CVs.

In the 'old days', CVs were posted to the company wishing to fill a vacancy. These days, CVs are *usually* emailed through to anyone and everyone. A lot of candidates searching for positions use the internet.

Always try and send your CV to a named individual.

- For security reasons, it is probably not a good idea to include your full address details, home telephone number, NI number etc. on your CV. Part of your home address, for example, Guildford, Surrey, as well as your email address and mobile telephone number should be enough. Alternatively, you could start by just putting down your email address as a point of contact.

- Once you have established a genuine link with the company that is hiring, more personal details can be given. So remember to hold back in the first instance, just to be on the safe side.

- Most people like children but avoid talking too much about them in your CV, unless you are applying for a job working with children.

- Don't use abbreviations or acronyms in your CV.

- Don't include a photograph of yourself in your CV.

- Avoid large unaccountable gaps in your CV.

- Avoid using too much bold type and too many capital letters.

- Keep your CV simple in appearance and avoid using too much creative detail, such as boxes, colour, fancy fonts and underlining.

- If you are 40 and over with say approximately 18 years' worth of work experience, try and keep your CV down to two pages – although three pages can sometimes be acceptable.

Avoid sending your CV out for a job opportunity if it is:

- Irrelevant for the role

- Too long

- Chaotic in its presentation

- Repetitious

- Badly typed

- Grammatically incorrect

- Too vague

- Disjointed with dates

- Lacking direction

- Inconsistent

- Out of date

4

CV layout

Basic CV preparation points to include for the individual with work experience:

- Name

- (Email address)

- Profile

- Work experience

- Training

- IT Skills

- Education

- Interests

- References available upon request

OR: For the school leaver or college leaver or graduate:

- Name

- (Email address)

- Profile

- IT skills

- Education

- Industrial work placement if applicable

- Work experience (including shop or restaurant work) while at school and/or university

- Interests

- References available upon request

5

Basic CV format

The suggested basic format of a Curriculum Vitae is given on the next two pages.

CURRICULUM VITAE

Name
(Email address)

Profile:

_____
_____
_____

Employment:

Company Name
Date started to present

Job title
Duties
_____
_____
_____
_____
_____
_____
_____
_____
_____
_____

Company Name
Date started to finish

Job title
Duties
_____
_____
_____
_____
_____
_____
_____
_____
_____

Company Name
Date started to finish

Job title
Duties

_____
_____
_____
_____
_____
_____
_____
_____
_____

Training: (if applicable)

_____

IT skills

_____
_____
_____

Education & Qualifications:

_____
_____
_____
_____
_____
_____

Interests:

_____
_____
_____

References available upon request

Name

6

CV comparison

If you have held several roles within the same company, it would be an idea not to put a separate company name heading and date for each role. If you do this a prospective employer might get the impression that you have had many jobs, that you can't settle and that you will 'continue' to job hop. Remember, most CVs are read at a glance. For this reason you might miss out on being invited for an interview. See Examples A and B.

Example A

Employment:

Same Company Ltd

Title/role August 2006– March 2009

_____
_____
_____
_____

Same Company Ltd

Title/role August 2005- July 2006

_____
_____
_____

Same Company Ltd

Title/role March 2004-July 2005

_____
_____
_____

Different Company Ltd   April 2002-February 2004

Title/role

_____
_____
_____

Different Company Ltd January 2000-March 2002

Title/role

_____
_____
_____

By presenting your CV this way, it is easier to see that you have worked for three different companies while at the same time it is possible to see that you have held five positions. Your CV therefore doesn't look as though you have an unsettled work record. As a result, you will stand a greater chance of being selected for an interview.

Example B

Employment:

Same Company Ltd   March 2004-March 2009

Title/role (August 2006– March 2009)
_____
_____
_____

Title/role (August 2005- July 2006)
_____
_____
_____

Title/role (March 2004–July 2005)
_____
_____
_____

Different Company Ltd   April 2002-February 2004
Title/role
_____
_____
_____
_____

Different Company Ltd   January 2000-March 2002
Title/role
_____
_____
_____
_____

7

School and college leaver CV examples

Suggested ways to present a CV if you are looking for a first job after leaving school or college.

James Jones
London SW11
jones@gmail.com

Profile: ————————————————————————————————————
——
——

Computer Skills: ——————————————————————————————————

Education:

Smithfield School. Hester Road, Clapham.
September 2002 - July 2009

A Level:

History (B)
Geography (C)
English (C)

GCSE:

English (A)
History (A)
Geography (B)
Art (B)
Maths (B)
Science (B)
IT (B)
French (B)

Employment: (Part-time while at school)

Clock House Sports Equipment Limited
September 2008 – February 2009

Sales Assistant
During my time working for this family owned sports shop I served customers. Gave advice to customers on different products and equipment. Dealt with new stock and assisted the manager with banking.

Anderson's Supermarket Limited
January 2008 – August 2008

Cashier
I mainly served customers, used the tills, cashed up and arranged the shelves

Interests

Sport
Computer games,
Playing the guitar

References available upon request

Susan Smith

smith@gmail.com

Profile: Bright, enthusiastic and hardworking junior keen to find an administration assistant's role within a busy and progressive company.

Computer Skills: _____

Education:

Eastside Tertiary College. Thames Road, Clapham.
September 2008 – July 2009

Junior Secretarial Course
Secretarial & Business Certificate - Pass

Robin Hood School. Beech Road, Clapham.
September 2002 - July 2008

GCSEs
English (B)
History (B)
Geography (C)
Art (C)
Maths(C)
Science (C)
I.T. (C)

Employment: (Part-time while at school and college)

Trendy Fashions Ltd
September 2008 - February 2009
Sales Assistant
Served customers, helped them choose new styles, dealt with new stock and assisted with banking.

Anderson's Supermarkets Ltd
January 2008 - August 2008
Cashier
Worked the tills, served customers, cashed up.

Interests:
Fashion
Ice-skating
Reading

References available upon request

CURRICULUM VITAE

Jessica Hudson
jh@gmail.com

Profile: I have an outgoing personality. I enjoy working with customers and am patient and helpful at all times.

Computer Skills: _____

Education:

Chalfont School. Lime Road, Brighton
September 2003 - July 2009

GCSEs
Science (B)
English (C)
History (C)
Geography (C)
Art (C)
Maths(C)
IT (C)

Employment: (Part-time)

Style Boutique January - May 2009

Sales Assistant
Served customers. Arranged window displays. Tidied stock. Helped order dresses and accessories.

Interests:

Fashion
Drawing
Swimming

References available upon request

A suggested way to present a CV if you are a graduate applying for a post that has nothing to do with the degree gained

Example **A** without the profile lacks direction

Example **B** with the profile gives focus to the CV

Example A

EDGAR HEARN
Date of Birth: 1/04/1988
Nationality: British

Home Address
Taunton Hall
Bridge Road
Brighton

Telephone 020 8123 4567
Mobile 007 007 0077
email: edgarh.com

EDUCATION

2006 – 2009   **Manchester University** BSc (Hons) Biology (First Class)

2004 – 2006   **Grant's High School A-Levels:** History, Biology & German

1999 – 2004   **Grant's High School GCSE:** Maths, French, German, Chemistry,
Biology, Latin, English Language, English Literature, History, Geography,
Art, Physics & Drama.

UNIVERSITY WORK EXPERIENCE

2007 – 2008   **Manchester University**
Events Coordinator
My duties included _____

_____
_____
_____
_____
_____
_____

2006 - 2007   **Manchester University**
Events Committee Member
Organized raffles, DJs _____

_____
_____
_____
_____
_____
_____

SCHOOL AND COLLEGE LEAVER CV EXAMPLES

EMPLOYMENT:

2007 – 2008   **The Crete Restaurant**
Assistant Manager
Helped run this busy family-owned Greek restaurant. My duties included
_____
_____
_____
_____
_____
_____

2006 - 2007   **Wood's Newsagents**
Sales Assistant
Serving customers at this family-run business _____
_____
_____
_____
_____
_____

ADDITIONAL ACHIEVEMENTS AND SKILLS

Languages: German fluent written and spoken

IT Skills: Word, Excel and PowerPoint

Achievements: Completed the London Marathon 2007
Duke of Edinburgh Award
St John Ambulance first Aid Course
Head Boy

REFERENCES:

Shirley Cluck
Waterways
Arundel

Paul Donald
Vision Zero
13, No Way
Bognor

Ms Duck
56, Bakers Dozen
Chamber Lane
Bognor

Example B

EDGAR HEARN

Motivated and enthusiastic graduate with excellent people skills who is a team player with the ability to work independently when required. I am determined to secure a progressive role within a successful event company where I can learn and also utilize my experience.

Location: Taunton
Email: edgarh.com

EDUCATION

2006 – 2009   **Manchester University** BSc (Hons) Biology (First Class)

2004 – 2006   **Grant's High School, A-Level:** History, Biology & German

1999 – 2004   **Grant's High School. GCSE:** Maths, French, German, Chemistry, Biology, Latin, English Language, English Literature, History, Geography, Art, Physics & Drama.

UNIVERSITY WORK EXPERIENCE – part time:

2007 – 2008   **Manchester University**
Events Coordinator
My duties included _____
_____
_____
_____
_____
_____
_____
_____

2006 - 2007   **Manchester University**
Events Committee Member
Organized raffles, DJs _____
_____
_____
_____
_____
_____
_____
_____

EMPLOYMENT part time during holidays:

2007 – 2008   **The Crete Restaurant**
                 Assistant Manager
                 Helped run this busy family-owned Greek restaurant. My duties included
                 _____
                 _____
                 _____
                 _____
                 _____
                 _____

2006 - 2007   **Wood's Newsagents**
                 Sales Assistant
                 Serving customers at this family-run business _____
                 _____
                 _____
                 _____
                 _____
                 _____
                 _____

ADDITIONAL ACHIEVEMENTS AND SKILLS

Languages: German fluent written and spoken

IT Skills: Word, Excel and PowerPoint

Achievements: Completed the London Marathon 2007
                    Duke of Edinburgh Award
                    St John Ambulance first Aid Course
                    Head Boy

PERSONAL DETAILS:

Date of Birth: 1 April 1988

Nationality: British

REFERENCES AVAILABLE UPON REQUEST

EDGAR HEARN

CV comparison for a school leaver

Example **A** is too fussy

Example **B** is the suggested correct way because it is easier to read

Example A

Maggie Thorpe
The Corner Shop
Hampstead
mthorpe.com
Tel (Home): 000 0
Tel (Mobile): 77777

Work experience *(Saturdays and school holidays - part time)*

	Company	Position
July 2008 – March 2009	*The Art Book Shop Ltd*	**Sales Assistant**, *served art materials and books to customers. Operated the tills and dealt with refunds.*
November 2007 – June 2008	*The Jean Shop Ltd*	**Sales Assistant**, *Served customers, cashed up, sorted stock and helped with general duties.*

Education

September 2002 – June 2009   St Hilda's School. West Road. Hampstead. NW3 HGN

A Levels in	
English & Art	A & B grades
GCSE's in	A
Biology	B
Maths	B
French	C
History	C
Chemistry	A
Art	C
Physics	B
English Language	A
English Literature	A

IT Skills - *Microsoft Word & Excel*
Interests - *I enjoy art, reading and music*

Example B

Maggie Thorpe

Email: *mthorpe.com*

Profile:
I am a quick learner, hard working and able to follow instructions effectively. I have strong computer skills and work well on my own as well as part of a team. I enjoyed English and Art at school. I am passionate about books and an avid reader. I am very keen to find a junior level administration role within a publishing company.

IT Skills: Experienced in Microsoft Word and Excel.

Education:

St Hilda's School West Road, Hampstead.
September 2002 – June 2009

A Level:
English (A)   Art (B)

GCSE:
English Language (A)
English Literature (A)
Art (C)
Biology (B)
Maths (B)
French (C)
History (C)
Physics (B)
Chemistry(A)

Part time work experience:

The Art Book Shop Limited   July 2008 – March 2009
Sales Assistant
Sold art materials and books to customers
Operated the tills and dealt with refunds

The Jean Shop Limited   November 2007 – June 2008
Sales Assistant.
Served customers
Cashed up, sorted stock and helped with general duties

Interests

Art
Reading
Music

References available upon request

8

General level CV examples

How to bring the profile on this CV to the point and incorporate the job roles.

Example **A** is too long and repetitious.

Example **B** is the suggested correct way because it is easier to follow and holds the reader's interest.

Example A

George Smith

10, Upton Street, London SW1
Contact Number: 007 000 00
Email: gsmith.com

Profile
Excellent accounts background working in the finance sector as a senior manager. I am very good at managing teams and working to very tight deadlines. I enjoy meeting targets and have led teams of up to 30 staff. I am very motivated and thrive when presented with a challenge. During the last 12 months my department has been learning a new computerised system. I personally organised the training workshops. I am very ambitious and keen to secure a senior management role within finance. I also

_____
_____
_____
_____
_____
_____
_____
_____
_____
_____

Employment

April 2006 – March 2009   **ABC Limited**
Manager of Finance

_____
Budgets ——
_____
_____
_____
_____
_____
_____
_____

January 2005- March 2006   **ABC Limited**
Assistant Manager of Finance

_____
_____
_____
_____
_____
_____
_____

Employment cont.

September 2003 - December 2004   **ABC Limited**
Finance Assistant

August 2001 – August 2003   **Global Financial Limited**
Administrator

August 2000 – August 20001   **PAYE Limited**
Junior Administrator

Education

Idaho University, 1997 - 2000
BSc (Hons) 2i - Business & Finance

South of England Business School, 1996
Business Diploma

Wilmington Boy's Grammar, 1995
A Levels: Law, Business Studies and Maths

Wilmington Boy's Grammar, 1993
GCSEs: Maths, English Language, English Literature, Business Studies, French, History, Geography, Physics, Chemistry, Biology

Personal Development
Management Training _____
Motivation Training _____
Sales Skills _____

IT Skills
Works, Excel, Power Point, Sage

Personal
Date of Birth   14th November 1978
Nationality   Swiss
Interests   Reading, cooking, golf, mountaineering and chess

References Are Available On Request

37

Example B

George Smith

London SW1
Email: gsmith.com

Profile:

A highly successful Accounts Specialist with an excellent track record of working at senior level within the financial sector. Extremely motivated with strong leadership qualities and the determination to succeed in the most demanding situations.

Employment:

ABC Limited September 2003 – March 2009

Manager of Finance
(April 2006 – March 2009)

Budgets

Assistant Manager of Finance
(January 2005- March 2006)

Finance Assistant
{September 2003 - December 2004)

Employment: (Continued)

August 2001 – August 2003   Global Financial Limited
Administrator

_____
_____
_____
_____

August 2000 – August 20001   PAYE Limited
Junior Administrator

_____
_____
_____
_____

Education:

Idaho University, 1997 - 2000
BSc (Hons) 2.1 - Business & Finance

South of England Business School, 1996
Business Diploma

Wilmington Boys' Grammar, 1995
A Levels: Law, Business Studies and Maths

Wilmington Boys' Grammar 1993
GCSEs: Maths, English Language, English Literature, Business Studies, French, History, Geography, Physics, Chemistry and Biology.

Personal Development Courses in:

Management Training _____
Motivation Training _____
Sales Skills _____

IT Skills:

Word, Excel, Power Point, Sage and various bespoke packages

Interests:

Reading, cooking, golf, mountaineering and chess

References available upon request

George Smith

How to improve a long and 'unsettled' CV.

Example **A** - The candidate has not settled into any role and has had too many jobs. There is too much repetition in the profile.

Example **B** is shorter, to the point and even though the candidate has moved positions, it is still possible to follow the experience gained without getting bored!

Example A

JUNE MAJOR
junemajor.com

PROFILE
I am a very ambitious and motivated person with strong accounting and administration skills. I am a strong team player also able to work as part of a team. I am extremely motivated and can cope remarkably well in highly competitive situations. I have excellent team building skills and a superb eye for detail. I am keen to find a role within a busy and productive company where my transferable skills can be put into action. I enjoy working towards a goal and will never leave a task incomplete. I am particularly interested in finding an accounts position within a busy department.

KEY SKILLS
Experience using various computer packages including _____

KEY QUALIFICATIONS

EMPLOYMENT HISTORY

Smalls Trading Ltd – Surrey - September 2008 – March 2009
Financial Assistant (Temporary)
Smalls Trading is a family run business specialising within the food and drink sectors. Most of

My duties included: _____

Let's Limited - London - June 2007 – August 2008
Financial Assistant (Temporary)
Let's is a printing company offering a full graphics service to the printing industry. My main duties were to ————————————————————————————————

Cushion Covers Ltd – London - April – May 2007
Financial Administrator (Temporary)
Cushion Covers is a soft furnishings company supplying to the property development sectors.
My ————————————————————————————————————

Postcard Limited – London – April 2006 – March 2007
Financial Administrator (Temporary)
Postcard Limited are a specialist graphics company. My role was to————————

———————————————————————————————————————
———————————————————————————————————————
———————————————————————————————————————
———————————————————————————————————————
———————————————————————————————————————

Postcard Limited – London – March 2005 – March 2006
Financial Assistant (Temporary)
My role was to————————————————————————————

———————————————————————————————————————
———————————————————————————————————————
———————————————————————————————————————
———————————————————————————————————————

I also held the following positions:

Financial P/A————————————————————————————

———————————————————————————————————————
———————————————————————————————————————
———————————————————————————————————————

Financial Secretary ————————————————————————

———————————————————————————————————————
———————————————————————————————————————
———————————————————————————————————————

Financial Assistant————————————————————————

———————————————————————————————————————
———————————————————————————————————————
———————————————————————————————————————

Financial Support—————————————————————————

———————————————————————————————————————
———————————————————————————————————————

Wooden Tops Limited – London - January 2005 – February 2005
Administration Assistant (Temporary)
Wooden Tops is a wood specialist company supplying to the furniture trade. My duties were to

———————————————————————————————————————
———————————————————————————————————————
———————————————————————————————————————
———————————————————————————————————————

Focus Limited – Suffolk – January 2004 – December 2004
Finance Assistant (Temporary)
Focus Limited is a camera company. My duties were to ——————————————

——————————————————————————————————
——————————————————————————————————
——————————————————————————————————
——————————————————————————————————

Hassock Limited – London – September 2002 – December 2003
Finance Administration (Permanent)
Hassocks Limited is a small family run engineering firm supplying to the car industry. My duties
were ——————————————————————————————

——————————————————————————————————
——————————————————————————————————
——————————————————————————————————
——————————————————————————————————

Media Limited – London – May 2002 – August 2002
Accounts Assistant (Temporary)
Media Limited is a publishing company. My duties were to————————————

——————————————————————————————————
——————————————————————————————————
——————————————————————————————————
——————————————————————————————————

Marsh and Spence Associates – London - February 2002 – April 2002
Accounts Administrator (Temporary)
Marsh and Spence is a firm of surveyors. My duties were to————————

——————————————————————————————————
——————————————————————————————————
——————————————————————————————————
——————————————————————————————————

Hair Today – Sussex - July 1997 - January 2002
Hairdresser and Beautician (Permanent)
Hair Today is a hair and beauty salon. My duties were to ————————

——————————————————————————————————
——————————————————————————————————
——————————————————————————————————
——————————————————————————————————

EDUCATION

Brighton College – Sussex - September 1995 – July 1997

Hairdressing and Beauty Diploma
RSA 1 and 2

Brighton School – Sussex – 1991 - 1995

GCSE:
English Language
English Literature
Maths
Geography
Art
History

PERSONAL DETAILS

Date of Birth 8th **June 197**9
Nationality: British
Marital Status: Single

Example B

JUNE MAJOR

junemajor.com

Hard working accounts administrator with excellent customer care skills seeks a demanding role as an Accounts Assistant within the financial sector.

EMPLOYMENT HISTORY

Smalls Trading Ltd September 2008 - March 2009
Financial Assistant (Temporary)
Smalls Trading is a family run business specialising within the food and drink sectors. Most of my duties included: —————————————————————————————————
———
———
———

Let's Limited June 2007 - August 2008
Financial Assistant (Temporary)
Let's is a printing company offering a full graphics service to the printing industry.
My main duties were to —————————————————————————————————
———
———
———

Cushion Covers Limited   April - May 2007
Financial Administrator (Temporary)
Cushion Covers is a soft furnishings company.
My duties were to —————————————————————————————————————
———
———

Postcard Limited March 2005 – March 2007
Postcard Limited is a specialist graphics company.
My positions and duties (temporary and permanent) were as follows:
Financial Administrator ————————————————————————————————

Financial Assistant ——————————————————————————————————

Financial P/A —————————————————————————————————————

Financial Secretary ——————————————————————————————————

Financial Assistant ——————————————————————————————————

Financial Support ——————————————————————————————————

Wooden Tops Limited January – February 2005
Administration Assistant (Temporary)
Wooden Tops is a wood specialist company.
My duties were ————————————————————————

Focus Limited January – December 2004
Finance Assistant (Temporary)
Focus Limited is a camera company
My duties were————————————————————————

Hassock Limited September 2002 – December 2003
Finance Administration (Permanent)
Hassocks Limited is a small family run engineering firm supplying to the car industry. My duties
were ————————————————————————————————————

Media Limited May 2002 - August 2002
Accounts Assistant (Temporary)
Media Limited is a publishing company. My duties were to ————————————

Marsh and Spence Associates February 2002 – April 2002
Accounts Administrator (Temporary)
Marsh and Spence is a firm of surveyors. My duties were to ——————————————

Hair Today July 1997 - January 2002
Hairdresser and Beautician (Permanent)
Hair Today is a hair and beauty salon. My duties were to ————————————

EDUCATION:

Brighton College Sussex 1995 - 1997
Hairdressing and Beauty Diploma
RSA Stages 1 and 2

Brighton School Sussex 1991 - 1995
GCSE: English Language, English Literature, Maths , Geography, Art, History

IT Skills: Word, Excel, Sage ————————————————————————

Interests: Cooking, sewing, fashion and beauty.

References: Available upon request.

June Major

An example of a CV for a graduate with limited work experience since graduation. The industrial work placement experience has been put to good use and this gives the CV more substance.

Also an example of a CV with the use of bullet points.

ANTONIA BLAIR

Guildford, Surrey
email ablair.co.uk

Profile

Marketing graduate with agency and industry experience keen to secure a challenging and demanding Account Executive role within a dynamic and successful integrated marketing agency.

Work Experience:

M&P Agency September 2008 to present

Junior Account Executive

Working on client accounts for Marks & Spencer, Habitat, Nestle, Honda
My duties include:
*   Attending meetings with clients and suppliers
*   Giving full support to the Account Managers and Directors
*   Writing briefs and ————————————————————————
*   Contacting the creative teams for ————————————————
*   Being responsible for full feedback to ————————————————
*   ————————————————————————————————————
*   ————————————————————————————————————
*   ————————————————————————————————————
*   ————————————————————————————————————
*   ————————————————————————————————————
*   ————————————————————————————————————

Any Company Ltd September 2006 to September 2007
(Industrial work placement)

Marketing Executive
As part of my degree I worked for this fashion house.
Any Company Ltd specialise in the design and distribution of ————————————

I was responsible for the following:

*   Assisted the Marketing Manager with the promotion of ————————————
*   ————————————————————————————————————
*   ————————————————————————————————————
*   ————————————————————————————————————
*   ————————————————————————————————————
*   ————————————————————————————————————
*   ————————————————————————————————————

Work experience while at school and university

J & K Shops Ltd - January 2005 - November 2006

Shop Assistant
My job involved serving customers, cashing up and ordering stock as well as ————————
——
——
——

Smith's Ltd - April 2001 - December 2004

Waitress
Duties included serving customers, taking in stock ————————————————————————
——
——

Education:

Newcastle University - 2004 2008
DA (llons) 2.1 in Marketing
Modules included International Marketing, Business Marketing & Advertising,.

Non Such School – 1997 - 2004
A Levels: A grades in: English, Biology and Business Studies
GCSEs: A&B grades in:
Maths, History, Geography, Physics, English Language, English Literature, Religious Education and Art

IT Skills: Word, Excel ————————————————————————

Interests: Reading, Sport, Design

References available on request

Antonia Blair

Christine Jones

Profile
I am a highly adaptable graduate with ——————————————————————————

IT Skills
Microsoft Office - Word, Excel, Power Point ——————————————————

WORK EXPERIENCE

R K Communications – PR Agency
Account Handler November 2008 - Present
I worked closely with the Senior Account Director on the following Accounts:

-
-
-
-
-
-
-
-
-
-
-

Get Smart - Marketing Agency
Office Administrator May - November 2008
Reported to the Marketing Director

-
-
-
-
-
-
-
-
-
-

Howard Services
Accounts Assistant April 2007 - May 2008
Reported to the Accounts Director

-
-
-
-

Asda Supermarkets
Office Administrator (Part-time then full time after university) November 2004 - March 2007
- _____
- _____
- _____
- _____
- _____

Howdy Services
Assistant to the Promotions Director (Part-time) February - November 2004
- _____
- _____
- _____
- _____
- _____

Asda Supermarkets
Retail Assistant (Part-time) May 1999 - January 2004
- _____
- _____
- _____
- _____
- _____

Education

Non Such University New Zealand 2002 – 2005
Bachelor of Marketing
Majoring in Marketing. Courses undertaken included _____

Buckingham Street High School 1995 - 2002
A Level equivalents in History, Biology and Art
GCSEs equivalents in 10 subjects including English and Maths

Further Training

Senior First Aid Training Course 2006

References available upon request

Christine Jones

Example of a standard letter to accompany a CV.

14 Sheep Way
Hurley
Sotheby
SNR 1TR

Ms L Jones
Office Manager
Another Toy Company Ltd
Plain Road
Sotheby
SNR TXV

21 June 2008

Dear Ms Jones,

I am very keen to apply for the role of Marketing Account Manager that your Company advertised in last Friday's edition of *The Daily News*.

The position is of great interest to me because I have spent the last three years working as a Marketing Account Manager for Pre School Toys Limited.

As you may be aware from the press, my company is relocating to Dubai and for this reason I am looking for a new position.

Please find attached a copy of my CV and I look forward to hearing from you at your earliest convenience.

Yours sincerely,

Harriet Smith

9

Deciding on the best sort of position

It is important to look for a job that will totally suit your situation.

You have just left school or college. You may be returning to the job market after having children or you could be a more mature candidate wishing to return to work because your family have grown up and left home. Whatever your situation, the role you seek should accommodate your circumstances.

It is very important to know what sort of company you may wish to work for and you should also have a general idea of the sort of job role you are seeking.

Some positions will require you to have transferable skills so sometimes it is better not to be too rigid with your requirements.

Some smaller companies require the candidate to have the ability to be 'several departments rolled into one'. For this you will need to be extremely flexible and also have the ability to multi-task.

Candidates sometimes worry about finding new employment once they are over a certain age. A date of birth doesn't need to be in a CV. However, more mature candidates often choose to leave their date of birth off their CV specifically to try and disguise their age. Your work experience will give an indication of your more mature years so it is a 'no win' situation.

Silent discrimination is quite common when it comes to age and little can be done about it.

Your older years will be obvious if you turn up for an interview wearing an outfit that makes you look like 'mutton dressed as lamb'.

For these reasons it is vital to work in an environment that relishes the experience of a more mature individual. Choose a company that will value your experience and input.

So you are single, getting close to 40 and looking for a new job and probably a rich partner! For this reason you may eye up your very attractive interviewer.

Don't work at getting the job because you fancy your boss. Yes, some bosses might be open to having an affair but once the affair is over you may also find that you are out of a job.

Take the job because you really want to do the job irrespective as to whether your boss looks like Quasimodo or George Clooney, Angelina Jolie or a pantomime dame!

If you are female, 35 plus, without children and newly-married, you may find that job offers don't come your way easily. A prospective employer could be concerned that you might want to start a family soon after joining the company. The interviewer won't be able to ask. It will be up to you to work hard at convincing the interviewer that you are the right person for the position because of your knowledge and experience.

If you are a parent coping with a child or children under the age of 13, the pressures of full-time work may not be for you.

Parents who have young children and want to work cannot use the school as a babysitting service in order to hold down a job successfully.

A lot of new parents say they are ready to start work again once their children/ child reaches 6 months – because the child can go to nursery! However, if your child is ill, who will look after your child?

Parents sometimes feel that they are ready to return to employment when their child reaches five years and has started school. The parent may feel able to work a full day because the child will be collected from school by a friend or family member when school finishes. What happens if your child becomes unwell? The answer is often 'My child is never unwell'.

Political correctness prevents the interviewer from asking the interviewee sensible and realistic questions. By avoiding certain topics during an interview it may seem easier to secure a position, but is it going to be possible to hold down the post successfully in the long term?

Most people have to work and usually for financial reasons. So, if you have young children and you are looking to secure a position make sure it is a role you can realistically do so your children don't suffer and your work colleagues don't feel that you are not pulling your weight.

It is better to take on a position that will provide you with the support you need when you need it. A job you know you can do.

When you have children, applying for part time work can often be the answer.

During the interview it will be possible to talk about home commitments without feeling uncomfortable.

If you are lucky enough to have good backup from family members, or from a couple of close friends, this should help, if the need arises.

Technology makes working from home very possible and a lot easier. Any company you apply to for a role where your work will be based from your home will call you in for an interview. When this happens, be prepared to follow the rules and have your interview techniques up to date, as the company will want to see that you have the ability to represent them in the correct manner.

If you have been out of the loop for a while, it is important to know that even the most informal interview should be taken seriously.

A prospective employer will look at you as 'a package', therefore you have to think – does my application tick all of the boxes? You may miss out to another candidate for the most basic reason. The simplest things can determine whether you get the job.

For example:

- Do you live near to the place of work?

- Is your journey to work easy?

- Will your journey to work be easy during the winter months?

- If the bus and train service is infrequent how would you get to work?

If there is no public transport near to the place of work you would need to drive and have a car. Can you drive?

Commitments outside the workplace can be a problem to those inside the workplace.

Are you studying at college in the evenings? If so how easy would it be for you to get to your course?

Do you have a childcare arrangement in place so you would have to leave the workplace at a set time?

The job market is so competitive and going for interviews is costly so whilst you may easily secure an interview, try and make sure you actually have a good chance of getting the role. Try not to take on an interview for a role that is more than you can realistically manage.

Even though the hours on a contract of employment may stipulate 9am to 5.30pm there is a lot of pressure in the workplace these days so staff are often expected to work longer hours. How would you realistically handle this situation?

Know how to deal with any questions that may relate to working the occasional extra time at the beginning or end of the day.

Questions that may help you decide on the sort of job role to look for:

- Why do you need to work?

- Do any of your friends have just the job you would like?

- What are you looking for in your new job?

- Who do you admire the most in the work place and why?

- Which well-known person do you aspire to be like?

- How related are your qualifications to the job you want?

- Is there a particular course you would like to do in your spare time?

- How related are your interests to the job you want?

- Do you have outside interests that can make up for lack of job satisfaction?

- Where do you see yourself in the next five years?

- What is your ultimate career ambition?

- What do you believe is realistically achievable?

10

Personal presentation

An interview costs time and money so you need to get your presentation right first time.

It's back to the old-fashioned way when it comes to your presentation for an interview.

Don't go to an interview dressed as though you are going to a wedding or a funeral.

Avoid patterned suits or suits that have short sleeved jackets. Avoid skirts with slits at the back or the sides.

Most people dress casually for work but it is important not to dress casually for an interview, no matter what the industry. The dressing down culture has to stop if YOU WANT that job.

The following are definitely out:

- Low-slung, frayed and ripped jeans with pants,

thongs or boxers showing. You may be applying for a role with a creative agency where this look is acceptable within the offices of work. However, the role may involve you visiting a corporate client such as a merchant bank or a firm of solicitors. The dress code on a daily basis within a creative agency environment may be extremely casual. However, you will need to avoid the casual look at an interview so that those conducting the interview will see you looking smart, knowing that you will come over well in every way should it be necessary to involve you when dealing with a client.

- Badly ironed, or designer style creased clothing. Once again this look can be misunderstood. The label may be high end but in the wrong environment, ie the workplace, you will not create the desired effect. Save this look for a night out clubbing.

- If you decide to wear a creased shirt or blouse under your jacket that should have been ironed, mark my words it will get noticed and you probably will not be invited back for a second interview. Badly creased clothes that are supposed to be ironed show a slovenly attitude.

- Boots with a skirt or trousers. This look just isn't smart enough for an interview and it won't matter how good the cut of the skirt or the trousers or how expensive the boots are. The look will be too casual.

- Bare legs with a skirt or trousers shows lack of effort and can make your presentation look down-market!

- Short skirts. This look is not at all suitable for an interview and you won't be taken seriously.

- Sandals. It doesn't matter how nicely polished your toenails are or whether your sandals are Jimmy Choo.

- High heeled shoes, stiletto's, platforms.

- Multiple earrings, studs and/or rings. No, take them off or out. One pair will be fine and they should not be big. Wear multiple earrings for your interview, then afterwards sit and wonder why you didn't get the job. If you are going for a job behind a bar in Camden then fine, maybe! But definitely not suitable for an office environment.

- Tongue and facial piercing. As above.

- Visible tattoos. As above.

- The 'unkempt hair look'. In moderation perhaps but a lot will depend on your age and also how extreme the style is.

- Spiky hairstyle. This hairstyle seems to be a favourite with young lads. You may be taking a risk if you wear your hair in this way for an interview. With less hair gel and a more moderate version of this style you may pass the dress code, but you could still be taking an unnecessary risk.

- Stubble. Quite simply, if you are going for an interview then have a proper shave. Why look as though you have spent the night out on the tiles?

- Roots. If you dye your hair make sure your natural roots are not showing. This look will ruin any smart appearance you may wish to achieve. So book yourself into your hairdresser and get your roots done before your interview.

- Cleavage on display is a no. What on earth are you trying to achieve! This look is definitely out.

- Tight trousers just do not look at all smart and send out the wrong signals. Avoid showing a visible panty line!

- A cardigan doesn't give the right image for an interview. No matter how expensive the cardigan, it just isn't going to be smart enough.

- Avoid wearing perfume or aftershave.

Don't go to an interview laden with luggage or carrier bags — find somewhere to leave these items. When nervous, the less there is to carry the better. Also, you don't want to look as though you are on the move.

Dress to suit your age.

Once you are over 25 you need to present yourself in a way that suits your years.

Basically there are dress codes for all ages. 20/30/40/50/60/70 plus. Every decade you clock up requires a presentation adjustment.

Women especially are absolutely paranoid about looking 'older' but we have to face getting and looking older at some point. If you are an older applicant looking for a new role your age will definitely go against you if you try to act and dress too young. When it comes to interviews, it is also important not to look frumpy, that never goes down well either. So do try and get the balance right.

Older men also need to avoid the pitfalls of dressing too young.

Remember, you will get that job if you are a good candidate. At 40, 50, 60 you simply can't 'act' 25! Just be yourself and you will secure the right position.

Ladies

- Invest in a tailored long-sleeved skirt suit or trousers suit. Choose a safe colour such as dark grey, navy or black then team the suit up with a smart white-collared shirt or blouse.

- Definitely avoid wearing a jacket in a heavy colour such as red, especially if you are over the size you would really like to be.

- Your skirt length should be on or below the knee.

- Wear natural coloured stockings/tights even during really warm weather.

- Polished classic plain black or navy court shoes with a heel of no more than two and a half inches.

- A standard size handbag the same colour as your shoes.

- Limited jewellery.

- Limited make up.

- Neatly cut, styled and combed hair.

- Keep your nails clean and tidy. Acrylic nails shouldn't be too long. Also, if you decide to wear nail polish then choose a natural colour.

Gentlemen

- Smart, nicely pressed suit either in dark grey, dark navy or black.
- White shirt with a standard collar that is the right fit.

- Standard width tie.

- Discreet cufflinks.

- Avoid heavily patterned ties.

- Classic styled, smart polished shoes in black.

- Black or very dark grey socks.

- Smart, conventional hairstyle.

- No jewellery except wedding/signet ring.

General

- Neat folder/portfolio.

- Take your own pen.

- Top coat if applicable.

- Ironed handkerchief or some new tissues.

- A small umbrella. Nothing can be worse than turning up for an interview looking like a drowned rat.

Remember, it's not just about what you wear, it's also about how you wear it.

11

Personal hygiene

This can be bit of a difficult subject to talk about but it does need to be dealt with.

Most candidates don't have a problem with personal hygiene. Unfortunately, in some cases, a small number of candidates do.

Nerves can make a person sweat more than usual. It might be a hot day and the candidate has rushed to the interview or the interview room may be warm on a cold day.

Whatever the circumstances, always make sure you apply a generous amount of deodorant and if possible make sure the fabric next to your skin is made of natural fibres.

There are plenty of ways to avoid body odour. If you smell, you will not get the job.

Surprisingly, many people who attend an interview also suffer from bad breath due to heavily spiced food, garlic, tobacco, dental problems, bad diet, or even alcohol.

Please don't eat spicy food the night before your interview. Apart from the fact that it could upset your stomach, how do you think garlic and onion 'fumes' will be welcomed during your interview the next day?

Cigarette breath can be equally off-putting. Just a couple of puffs on a fag before your interview, that is all you need to do to create offensive breath. So it is best not to have a cigarette before your appointment. If you must smoke, remember to use a breath freshener immediately afterwards.

Never chew gum during an interview.

If you have bad breath because of dental problems, it is important to see your dentist and get the problem sorted out quickly.

Some people have a problem with bad breath because they don't eat properly.

Tea or coffee on an empty stomach can also make the breath smell unpleasant.

Don't drink alcohol the night before your interview.

Apart from the fact that you won't want to have a hangover the next day, the day of your interview, alcohol breath can be just about the worst smell to give off at an interview. It will also give off a worrying message about you.

If you have an interview in the morning, eat breakfast beforehand and keep a packet of extra strong mints in your pocket so you can have one just before your interview.

An interview costs time and money. If you choose to ignore these basic guidelines, you will be wasting your time and money.

12

Communicate

Job searching can create huge emotional tensions. Spare a few minutes to think about those closest to you when you are looking for a job, especially if they are living with your stresses and anxieties.

If you feel comfortable about this idea, why not involve a member of your family, a partner or close friend with certain elements when it comes to the preparations for your job hunt? Sometimes, useful comments can come from the most unlikely quarters.

If you can, talk about how your job hunting is making you feel – try and offload any anxieties.

Discuss your planned interview techniques. Role-play if possible.

Ask for an opinion about your interview outfit and how you plan to present yourself.

If you can, get feedback as you compile your CV.

Try and view your search for a job as if it is a project.

Some people even say that they feel excited about looking for a job.

Your enthusiasm may not go that far but sharing how you feel could be a positive step towards making you feel less tense and more reassured.

13

Time keeping

It is very important to always be on time for an interview.

If you are late for an interview it won't matter how well you perform after being late, the chances of you being offered the job will be greatly reduced.

- Always check out precisely where the company is situated well before your interview. If possible, visit the location.

- Arriving with ten minutes to spare before the interview is due to commence will not allow you enough time. Unforeseen situations may occur such as problems with parking your car.

- Avoid telephoning the company where your interview is being held to make parking arrangements.

- Get to your interview with plenty of time to spare and have enough loose change on you for the parking meter if that is the only method of parking available. If possible use a car park or a free parking area.

- An interview can sometimes last for quite a long time, especially if it is going well. You wouldn't want to cut your appointment short because your meter was running out of time. This would kill the interview, make the whole exercise a waste of time and make you look unprofessional.

- Don't park in the staff car park unless you have expressly been given permission in advance to do so. However, best to avoid doing this as you wouldn't want to draw attention to yourself if your car was to get blocked in. A parking problem could result in your interview being interrupted, which would be most embarrassing for you.

- If your interview is being held in a large office building, you will need to leave plenty of time to get through security. Commissionaires can be notoriously slow, there is bound to be a queue of people going through the security check so allow an extra 30 minutes.

- If you are catching a train, make sure you allow at least an hour extra for your journey to cover cancellations. Delays due to rail works can often occur when travelling by train to an interview outside the rush hour period.

- The same rule should apply if you are travelling by car. School runs from the early part of the afternoon can cause traffic chaos.

- Always make sure you have enough petrol in your car and always know where you are going to park in advance. It pays to leave plenty of time for your journey so that if you have a problem with your car, for example a puncture or flat battery, at least you will have the chance to get a taxi.

- If you are 15 minutes early, this will be an acceptable time to arrive at reception ready and composed for your interview.

- As a reminder, avoid eating out the night before an interview. A dodgy stomach due to a bad meal may mean you become too unwell to attend your appointment. This could lead to a change of day and time being difficult to rearrange. The company may not take kindly to having the interview process delayed and you could end up missing the job opportunity altogether.

14

How to stay calm before and during an interview

This is always going to be a difficult one. Some people never get nervous during interviews and some people go to pieces. We can be our own worst enemy when it comes to nerves before an interview.

Some guidelines to help calm your nerves:

- Be enthusiastic about your interview.

- Try not to start doing your research the night before your interview.

- Totally research the company well in advance.

- Make a few notes that you can refer to well before your interview.

- Try not to take notes with you to the actual interview.

- Make sure, well in advance, that your interview outfit is ready to wear.

- Make sure your portfolio is in order if you are taking one.

- Avoid getting your hair done on the day of your interview.

- Arrive in plenty of time for your interview.

- Visit the company's location a day or two before the interview.

- Take a lucky item that is small and can be kept in your pocket.

Most people try what they think is their best at an interview but you need to know your best is definitely good enough.

If you know you have tried your best because you have followed the guidelines and you don't get the job then it wasn't meant to be.

A third of your time can be spent at work so when you attend an interview it is important to feel comfortable with the job, the surroundings and the people.

Always try and have your interviews during peak office hours and that way you will be able to get an impression of the working environment. Hopefully, the receptionist will make you feel at ease and you will be able to observe quite a lot from your seat in the reception area.

If, say after the second or third interview stage, you are invited out for lunch as a formality by your prospective boss or company, don't drink any alcohol.

You may relax too much, end up saying the wrong things and miss out on a definite offer.

Remember, even at this late stage, the final decision could be between you and someone else. So stay calm and remain professional.

15

What to say during an interview and how to project your personality

The aim of the interviewer is to fill the role with the ideal candidate at the earliest possible opportunity.

The aim of the interviewee is to get the ideal role at the earliest possible opportunity.

Preparation is key, so:

- Make sure you have studied the job description fully before your interview.

- Base your prepared questions on what you have read from the job description, the company's website and brochure.

- If you feel nervous ask yourself why?

Make every effort not to feel nervous because the more often you do feel nervous, the more times you will have to go through the interview process. Why give the job opportunity to someone else because you have allowed your nerves to ruin your interview technique?

- Always maintain good eye contact with the person who is interviewing you.

- Deportment is very important if you want to make the right impression. How you carry yourself will be noticed. Stand to attention when you are being greeted.

- A good firm handshake is vital when you first meet the person or people who will conduct your interview and remember the handshake at the end of the interview too.

- Make sure you sit upright during the interview.

Don't slouch as you will give the impression that you are not at all interested in the role that is being discussed or anything else for that matter.

The ideal interview scenario will be if your interview is one to one.

However, if you are faced with a panel interview, don't be put off by this. Try and remain composed and answer all the questions you are asked clearly and concisely.

Examples of questions and answers for the less experienced candidate

- Question: Why do you want a job for example in Marketing?

- Answer: Because I studied Marketing at university and completed an industrial placement for 12 months with Fragrances Limited, a cosmetic company. I held the position of Marketing Assistant and my duties included....

Good continuation between interviewer and interviewee.

- Question: Why do you want a job in Marketing?

- Answer: Because I studied History at university.

- Question: What has History got to do with Marketing?

- Answer: Eh... I don't know!

Without meaning to you have ended the interview.

- Question: Why do you want a job in Marketing?

- Answer: Because after graduating in History I worked on a temporary contract for a marketing agency as a Marketing Assistant. I realise that Marketing is the career path I wish to follow. I will be enrolling to study a diploma in Marketing during my spare time.

Good continuation between interviewer and interviewee.

Knowing about a relevant course will also open up the conversation between you and the interviewer.

Nerves can play havoc no matter how confident the individual.

Wanting to make the right impression can make a person nervous.

It is important to remember that the interviewer can be just as nervous as the interviewee, so a little light-hearted conversation can hold the interview together thus avoiding pregnant pauses. This is where talking about hobbies and interests can sometimes 'break the ice'.

If you are nervous, hopefully the interviewer will pick this up from you quickly and home in on your interests. This technique can really make an interviewee open up. But, once again a lot will depend upon how much the interviewer wants to or is able to make you feel relaxed.

If the interviewer makes you feel relaxed, don't fall into the trap of being too familiar by talking a lot, telling jokes or laughing too much; that will lose you the job. Just carry on asking and answering questions in a professional yet friendly way. Always remember to listen too.

- Always ask questions at an interview.

- Make sure the questions you ask are intelligent!

- Even if you think you may know the answer to the most obvious questions, it still pays to ask. This will show that you are interested.

- Plan your questions well before the interview.

If during the interview you are asked what your ambitions are, give an answer that directly fits the role you are applying for.

For example:

- You could say that you are keen to settle into the position and grow with the company.

- If you come over as being over ambitious or if you are keen to ask about promotion prospects during the interview, it may be viewed that you will not settle into the role.

It is important to be enthusiastic about progression but go easy or you may not be called for a second or third interview.

- Always let the interviewer lead and don't interrupt or talk too quickly.

Sometimes, if you tell the interviewer you feel nervous, a short conversation can be created on the subject and before you know it you feel fine. This will of course depend on the person who is interviewing you.

How to deal with the strength and weakness question

- Try and focus on your good points. Avoid giving specific negative points such as bad time-keeping, impatience, preference to working alone.

- Instead turn one of your strengths into a weakness, for example, you could say you find it difficult to leave a task until it has been completed or that you are an early riser and are often the first one to arrive at work.

- Have the means to demonstrate how well you can work under pressure and to strict deadlines.

Some organisations don't always indicate that they are likely to test the candidate.

- Be prepared for any unexpected test situations.

- Take your favourite pen as you may need to do a written test.

Sometimes prospective employers want to see that you have neat and legible handwriting. Handwriting can say a lot about a person.

If you are going for an interview with a large structured company, you will probably be tested. It is important to find out as much as you can about the format of the test(s) via your recruitment consultant or the HR contact well before your interview.

Relocation

If you are going for interviews in a new area, for example you are moving from Manchester to London, know where you will be staying. You will be asked this question at an interview. Find a friend that you know you can stay with in an area close to where you are attending your interview. It won't do to say you will 'find somewhere to stay' if you get the job.

If it is a choice between you relocating and not knowing where you might stay and another candidate who knows where they will be staying, the other candidate will probably get offered the role.

Answer the question with an answer

- Try to create a short conversation around your answers but don't ramble on.

- Candidates have often lost out on job roles due to too much talking and by going off on tangents.

- Don't read from your CV. This can look as though you don't know much about yourself or that you may not be telling the truth about yourself.

If you want to take notes throughout the interview, do ask first. Sometimes it is best not to produce note pads, pens etc when first arriving for an interview. You may even find that it is not necessary to take notes at all.

Some people think handshaking is old-fashioned, but it is not.

- Handshakes are exceedingly important, they can tell a lot about one's strength of character.

- So practise your handshake. Don't go over the top by giving a knuckle crusher but try and give a short, firm handshake. Practise on your friends or a member of your family.

- There can be nothing worse than giving a limp, damp-palmed handshake. If you suffer from sweaty palms due to nerves, dry them discreetly, and I mean discreetly, on something such as a handkerchief. Don't let the interviewer catch you wiping your hand on your trousers or skirt!

- Give a firm handshake with good eye contact and a friendly smile.

During each interview, it is very important to keep the questions flowing, to look interested and to be enthusiastic.

Never be complacent as there is no guarantee you will get the job just because you get invited for a second or third interview with the same company.

- If your second or third interviews are with different people, treat each of the interviews as though you are visiting the company for the first time and ask each person who interviews you plenty of questions, even if they are the same questions you have already asked a different interviewer.

- Otherwise interviewer B may say to Interviewer A that he (she) thought you were a quiet candidate who lacked interest in the role. This conclusion could be reached if you failed to ask Interviewer B enough questions during the second interview.

You may have thought it unnecessary to ask questions the second time round because you knew the answers from the first interview with interviewer A. By not asking all of your interviewers questions, you are wasting an interview opportunity.

- Interviewer A and interviewer B will disagree about your application and you probably won't get the job.

Interviewer B will think you are a quiet reserved applicant lacking interest in the role. Interviewer A will think you are outgoing and friendly but will have fresh doubts about your application based on the comments from Interviewer B.

Companies like to feel you will 'belong' to them

So if you have dedicated interests outside work that could affect your commitment to working the occasional overtime because of a company deadline, you may have to give up those interests, or face not getting the job.

For example, you may need to attend a course that starts at 6.30 a couple of evenings a week. The course may have nothing to do with work, maybe you are learning how to swim or play the guitar.

Don't talk about any dangerous sports you may do in your spare time as this could go against your application. You won't come over as being macho or clever, just a potential liability. Give them up!

It is very important to say good things about your present and any previous employers

Company information is confidential. Remember this when you are giving your reasons for looking for new employment. If, for example, your present company is in financial difficulties, or your bosses don't get on and are always arguing or your married boss is having an affair, or he/she has a drink problem, keep this information or anything similar to yourself.

A lot of people choose where they want to work and the role they wish to do.

Some people seek out a new job because they feel they have out-grown their role, or because they feel disillusioned with the role.

Whatever your reason for choosing to 'move on', never talk badly about the company you are thinking of leaving.

During an interview, the interviewer will make up his or her mind about you very quickly so your application is less likely to be viewed favourably if you say negative things about any of your present or previous employers.

The interviewer needs to feel that you are honourable, trustworthy and loyal.

If while being interviewed you say that you are looking to leave your job because you have not been promoted, this could reflect badly on you. It could mean you actually did not do a good job and that you were therefore not worth the promotion or that your lack of experience meant you were not ready to be promoted.

Similarly, if a gripe with your salary is another reason for looking for a new job, it may be viewed that you were not worthy of the salary increase.

To talk about having a 'bad boss' or to talk about general disruption in the office is not a good thing to do either.

It costs a lot of time and money for a company to employ a member of staff. The commitment therefore has to work both ways.

If you are leaving because you didn't get on with your boss, don't mention this at an interview because it could come across that YOU are the one who might not be easy to get on with.

It always pays to remember that the business world can be quite 'closed'.

For example, imagine you go for an interview with a marketing company and the person conducting the interview knows your company or indeed your boss, or the interviewer may be fishing for company information. The interviewer won't tell you this, he or she will test your level of loyalty and you won't necessarily be aware that this is happening.

So, stick to the golden rules, talk positively about the role you are doing in your present job, the vacancy, hobbies, interests etc and when asked about your company just say it's an excellent place to work but that you are ready to move on, or something similar.

Feedback can actually be worth its weight in gold if you are unsuccessful in getting the role after an interview.

Always get feedback so you don't make the same mistake in your next round of interviews.

16

Marketing yourself

You may decide to use an employment agency to help you find a job.

However, you may also decide to apply directly to companies yourself. There are two ways of doing this:

- Either by applying in response to an advertisement.

- Or by targeting a select number of companies 'cold' that are of particular interest to you. These companies will not necessarily be advertising vacancies.

Always check that your CV is absolutely up to date. These days, there is no excuse for sending an out of date CV to a company.

When it comes to targeting companies 'cold', don't select too many at a time. Start with 10 companies until you reach a conclusion then target 10 more.

This will stop you from feeling disillusioned and will also prevent duplication and confusion.

- Keep a record of notes and comments from each interview in a file. This will give you a sense of progression.

- When targeting a company 'cold', it is always important to get the name of the person at the company who is in charge of receiving CV's.

- Get the contact's email address too.

Make sure your CV is received and get your CV noticed.

- Send your CV by email with a covering letter.

- Also send your CV by post with the same covering letter.

The reason for this duplication is quite simple. Firstly, sometimes not all emails are read by the recipient, they can also go to Spam. Secondly, as most CV's are emailed a nicely presented CV and covering letter sent by post will definitely get noticed! At least you will be covered if you send your CV by both methods.

- Always address all correspondence to the named individual.

- Avoid sending your correspondence to 'Whoever this May Concern', or to 'Human Resources' or to 'The Office Manager'.

The letter should be a short introduction briefly outlining what you have to offer as your accompanying CV will be explanatory.

Once a few days have passed, telephone any of the companies who have not responded to make sure your CV has been received... then wait.

Hopefully, you will get positive replies from the companies you have approached.

If one of the companies you have approached yourself contacts you and they invite you in for an informal interview, how do you handle the situation?

- Remember, any company who contacts you as a result of your direct contact will have seen something on your CV that is of interest.

- The company may not have put together a job description, so you will probably not have an idea of the salary or the duties.

- Don't let that put you off. Treat the informal chat as though it is a serious interview.

- Use the opportunity to really project yourself and your skills well. Do plenty of research and attend the interview with PURPOSE.

During the interview, it may be that the company will create a job description based on your skills, the salary will then follow and as long a it is more or less in line with your previous salary and the company's budget, all should be concluded positively.

It is better to be flexible with your salary expectations and the overall duties that may be required. If you are flexible you will stand a better chance of getting a job offer.

The great thing is you will have got in before anyone else and if you are suitable the company may decide not to advertise the role and instead offer the position to you.

It is important to have a disciplined mind when looking for a job.

- You need to be mentally and physically prepared before starting the interview process.

- Cut back on comfort food and if you don't belong to a gym then take up walking if you can.

- Aim to be fit and ready to Get That Job!

- Set aside an allocated number of hours each day for your job hunt.

- Get up early, at a fixed time, and do some form of exercise, walking, gym, swimming or whatever you can manage.

- Then work on your applications and research for a couple of hours.

- Stop for lunch then resume your search for a further couple of hours.

- Switch off and do something different for the rest of the afternoon and evening so you don't burn yourself out.

If you have a quiet personality consider the best way to boost your communication skills and confidence levels.

For example:

- When you go shopping try and talk to the cashier who may be serving you, even if you only mention the weather.

- If you find yourself in a crowded room and you don't know anybody then try initiating a conversation with the person next to you.

- As long as you are in a safe and secure environment, try and create a conversation as often as possible; this should help you feel more confident when speaking to people during an interview situation.

- If you have the funds, enrol on a weekend drama course.

Do everything you can to project your personality during an interview.

When doing research on companies, gather as much information from companies' websites' sales brochures and the press. Don't forget, the library can also hold a wealth of relevant information.

You may not necessarily get a job just because a friend or relative works for the company you are applying to.

So, always aim to get a job on your own merit.

17

Salary expectations

It is always best not to mention your salary expectations during an interview.

- Wait until the person who is interviewing you brings the subject up.

- When asked about your salary expectations, don't say you need a certain amount then talk about your bills, rent, mortgage etc.

- A salary is based on what the job is worth and not the cost of your outgoings.

- If you are asked directly to give your salary requirements, don't say a fixed figure of £30,000. Rather, say around £30,000. Then if the role is paying £28,000 or £32,000 you won't be too far off the mark.

- Try and show reasonable flexibility whether your salary expectations are £100,000 or £20,000.

- If the salary for the role is lower than you were hoping, don't show your disappointment or say the salary isn't enough.

- Don't lie when you are asked about your earnings. You will get found out if you say your salary is more or less than it actually is.

- Don't dictate salary at an interview.

After interviews with other companies, the lower salaried role might be the very role you decide you like the most. So, if you dismiss the opportunity too quickly, it will be very difficult to back track. You might not even be invited for a second interview because your attitude first time round regarding the salary would have indicated disappointment. The company would presume you are no longer interested in the role.

- A good candidate will show interest in the role and its content before the salary.

- Try to remain positive and focused because a lower salary can sometimes mean a better job.

- If you start on a lower salary, you may find that you will qualify for a good salary increase upon satisfactory completion of your probationary period.

Try not to keep talking about how good you would be for the role and how much of an asset you would be to the company. Don't blow your own trumpet just to prove you are worth a higher salary. In the end, if you are given the role, will all of your talking actually mean you can do the job?

If you start your new job on a slightly lower salary, you may be under less pressure to perform perfectly in your new role from day one.

You may find you are able to settle into the role more easily and do the job better. Also the right support is more likely to be at hand.

You may also qualify for certain training courses which could lead on to a more defined career opportunity.

Sometimes the salary level does not always indicate greater job involvement.

A few years ago there was little salary variation for similar roles. These days there can be a salary difference of a few thousand pounds for similar roles.

18

Reference details

Your prospective employer may wish to request reference details from individuals other than the ones you may have chosen to mention in your CV.

- When seeking a new role, it is very important to make sure that your contacts for reference details are up to date.

- Make sure you have had very recent contact with the person who will be giving you a reference. This is important because your contact could quite easily be on holiday or away from work for some other reason.

- Delayed references can hold up the start date process.

- Keep checking to make sure your referee is still

working for the same company.

Depending on the size of a company, sometimes references can only be available through the HR department of a company.

- If a personal reference is requested then make sure your contact is easy to locate.

A few years ago references were only ever done by post. This would give a candidate time to follow things through. Now, due to technology, references requests can be made more immediately.

- It is only polite to keep your referee in the loop regarding any job progress you make.

19

School or college leavers attending interviews for the first time

Whether you have just left school, or are a new graduate, if you lack work experience and you are presented with the opportunity of some work, ideally paid, then seize the opportunity – even if it isn't in your chosen field. It is very important to have work experience in your CV as this will help you get to where you want to be when it comes to any future applications.

Try not to feel daunted by the interview process.

Treat every single interview opportunity seriously.

Believe in yourself and you will get a job.

You may have little or no interview experience so if you are looking for your first permanent role in an office for example, make sure you do plenty of research. Try and familiarise yourself with an office environment. Make sure you keep your computer skills up to date while you are job hunting.

Whether you are looking for work in a shop, an office, a garage, a hairdressing salon or anywhere else, you will need to be prepared for all of your interviews. Try and follow the personal presentation and appropriate CV guidelines in this book as well as many of the other tips that are mentioned.

Remember to:

- Wear a suit for all of your interviews.

- Have a nicely presented CV.

- Do your research.

- Think of some questions.

- Always be on time.

Go to your interview with **PURPOSE**.

Summary

Just because you have a job it doesn't mean you can't be replaced! Remember to look after your job once you are lucky enough to get it because many people will be after your role.

So when you start your job – guard it with your life!

- Work hard

- Don't be the first to leave at the end of the day

- Avoid becoming complacent

- Keep up a smart dress code

- Always be on time

- Look interested

- Respect your boss

- Always be a good team player

- Meet your deadlines

- Don't suggest a salary increase or bonus

- Use office time wisely

- Avoid using office equipment for personal matters

- Always be discreet

A lot of people have said that if they left their job and then saw it advertised, there is a good chance that they would want to apply for the position again!

Checklist

It is always a good thing to have a check-list when going for interviews because when one is under pressure the most obvious things get forgotten.

For example

- Suit, interview outfit from the dry cleaners.

- Company name, interview address, telephone number and directions.

- Full name of interviewer.

- Your CV - in a folder just in case you need to present it.

- A copy of the job description – just in case you are asked to refer to it.

- Portfolio containing examples of work - if applicable.

- Pen

- Small note pad

- Mobile phone (do remember to switch it off before your interview).

- Certificates - if applicable.

- Driving Licence - if applicable.

- Passport - if applicable.

- Train/bus pass.

- Petrol.

- Change for parking.

- Small umbrella.

- Polish shoes.

- Check personal presentation.

-

-

-

Interview feedback

- ➢ Company _____
- ➢ Date _____
- ➢ Contact _____
- ➢ Title _____
- ➢ Feedback _____

  _____

  _____

Your comments _____

*   *   *

- ➢ Company _____
- ➢ Date _____
- ➢ Contact _____
- ➢ Title _____
- ➢ Feedback _____

  _____

  _____

Your comments _____

➤ Company _____

➤ Date _____

➤ Contact _____

➤ Title _____

➤ Feedback _____

  _____

  _____

Your comments _____

*   *   *

➤ Company _____

➤ Date _____

➤ Contact _____

➤ Title _____

➤ Feedback _____

  _____

  _____

Your comments _____

Notes